Lesson's

Totukani Amen II

Inner Alchemy's Publishing
Chicago, IL

First Edition

ISBN 978-0-9961266-2-5

Published by
    Inner Alchemy's Publishing (Inner Alchemy's)
    332 S. Michigan Ave.
    Ste 1032-C141
    Chicago, IL 60604-4434
    info@inneralchemys.com
    www.inneralchemys.com

Printed in the United States of America

There is entirely nothing wrong with reflection;

There is entirely nothing wrong with moving pass the illusion which was one's life

~ Priest Amen II

CONTENTS

Lesson 1

The Outward Projection
of the Ego

∞

A lot of listeners should know. I get emails and all the time, asking me, telling me that we have some great metaphysicians, we have great historians, we have people of all walks of life giving out this type of information, but yet it is not practical. I cannot after listening to a show, after reading their 1,000 page book, I cannot go out and pretty much do anything to better my life outright. Out of the hours spent listening out of the hours spent trying to do what these individuals say to do, for this manifestation to happen, in the end it could be practically looked at as a waste of time.

Throughout these lessons I'm going to show you directly as we move through these series how to manifest and literally do this in the physical reality what you have been wanting and waiting to do all your life. Now hopefully, if I have done my job correctly, you will see it is not that hard as your enemy or your adversary or as the yin to your yang wants you to think. They want you to think it is very difficult. They want you to think that you are unable to do anything. So pretty much you wake up every day, work your 9 to 5, maybe if you can save enough maybe go on a trip maybe once a year, two years or so. Eventually you have children and you are raising these children and sit back and rock on a rocking chair and eventually you die. I think that's not the way life is actually supposed to be led. It is for some people, but for the most part, those that I'm speaking to its not.

What is the ego? The ego is some form of pride. The ego stops manifestations unwillingly. Ego, if to be basic, you step on someone's shoes and you know you did it and instead of saying I apologize, you feel internally that it's not really worth it. They're really not worth it. And some would even express outwardly to the person afflicted that "yeah I stepped on your shoes, what are you doing to do about it? This is a very basic example.

People are living in overpopulated surroundings, and many suffer from a form of internal escapism because things get so tragic in their lives, crazy things are happening here, crazy things are happening there, so they want to escape from this reality and especially if you are into metaphysics or deep into spirituality, you want to leave this planet, go to the Sirius Galaxy, Heaven or some other place from here because you feel hopeless. Ego tends to populate ill will towards others; whenever someone has treated you wrong, whether there are time in your past where someone has treated you wrong when it is factual and actual their fault. But instead of moving past this or even forgiving them you harbor it, internalize it inside and you beat yourself up because of something someone has done to you. But this is something that you haven't even done to yourself. This is something they have done to you and you are beating yourself up because of it. And yet you have no control of something like that. Someone could do something to you tomorrow. You have no control over it; yet one of the main things that I would like to express is that this reality is not real. What do you mean it's not real? Yes, you feel things in this reality because it meant for you to feel things in this reality. That is the point of this reality is for you to feel things good or bad, to feel things up high or down low, in essence to experience life.

Also the point of this reality is to either do two things, for you to express love or show expressions that are non–love. When you see evil people, it's not that they show hate, there is no such thing as hate. Only thing there is in this entire universe is love and things that do not show love. That is it. There is nothing else. All of these other words, all of these other things that people come up with are just putting complications on things that are very simple. The more you look at it, the enemy of humanity if you want to call it that, tries to give you very complex scenarios and try to pass it off as simple. But in reality, most of the indigenous people of the world have been living very simple, but to the adversary it is extremely complex.

For example, there was a person, a friend of mine I met a while ago and she was always very confused about life, confused almost about everything and she had seen how in my life how I had never had any issues, any problems. I live life in a very peaceful way and it's always been like that once I understood certain basics of this reality. And so she says how do you do this? I said to her just be, Just relax, stop thinking about all the crazy stuff, just let and go and be. And literally something so simple was super complex for her to do. And so we have to get out of being bombarded and believing what the world says is okay and what it redundantly does in its overly made complex actions daily. This complexity is going to eventually drive you insane. The matrix movie was trying to show you something very important, specifically the matrix 1 for those who have not seen it, the matrix was trying to show you that what you believe to be reality reality is not real. That's the basic thing. That's the thing that is obvious. The next thing they were trying to show you is concerning the Smiths. First during scenes throughout the movie when a random bystander seen Neal or one of his comrades, Smith would take over and all of a sudden you see Smith and he is chasing them or trying to shoot them. But the fact of the matter is this; they were showing you something so evident like that, because they feel that you are unintelligent so much so that you would not get it.

What do I mean? The Smiths were actually portraying the adversary of this reality. First, let me say this is the reality of the dead. What…. Of the dead? Yes, of the dead. They do not want you to wake them up. They do not want you to tell them anything that makes sense, nothing, absolutely nothing. If you say the sky has chemical-trails (ie., chemtrails also see geo-engineering) that most of what you see aren't clouds I in the sky. They will say "what you talking about? You're crazy." They don't want you to open up minds to any possibility. Now the universal creator of all will awaken those few at a time that they need to be awakened. But some people are literally permanently dead. And this is something that those in the conscious community and those that are truly spiritual have yet to come to realization, that we have been bombarded with this super- hero complex that everybody can be saved. Everybody can do this and do that, everybody can open their minds. But the fact of the matter is that it has never been that way since the beginning of time. Everyone has never done everything and one must come to this conclusion especially at this time in this reality when there is so much at stake.

A lot of you all listening today are what is considered indigo children, crystal children, star seeds, or whatever else you want to come up with, whatever else fancy term you want to call it. But the fact is that in reality, it means you were sent here for a purpose. So, you were sent here for whatever you came from, for a purpose. Let's say your purpose was to lead the ying against the yang, or the light vs. the darker, or the darker vs. the light, that was your purpose. And instead you became a school teacher or a grocery bagger and that's what you did till you left from here. You were just sent here to be let's say the ruler of the world and instead you were an apple orchard picker. Okay, what is that? Now does that mean that there is anything wrong with being a school teacher, no not at all. Is there anything wrong with being a grocery bagger? No, there isn't anything wrong with any of that at all. But the fact of the matter is that it's something wrong for you to be doing it, because you're special. I'm not going to get into certain topics prematurely because lesson 1 deals with the ego. But in further lessons we will get into all types of topics that deal with all types of things that I will do my best to make as simple as possible and it will be so easy to understand. It is like wow, why didn't I think about that before.

4

Now let me get back into the matrix a bit. So, in the matrix what they are trying to show you is how your adversary can go in and out of bodies and of course if the matrix was done how they really wanted to show it when a Smith went inside of a body, the body would not change shape or anything. It would be that same person, a female, a young child, an older man, or whatever it may be. It would stay that way and the person would start acting crazy or in a way that is suspicious or starting to act in a way that literally is forcibly ill toward whomever the focus is on. But they felt that was a little too complex for the average person to understand. Even when they just put it out plainly, most people just don't get it. Such as when you go somewhere and you are just chilling, relaxing and a person will come out the blue and just mess with you and try to mess up your day and you're like where in the heck did they come from? What is this? They were inhabited by for arguments sake let us call a Smith, that's just a very generic what you call humorous connotation on that particular subject. But it is real, it is reality.

Why isn't more information about what governors us, or this reality more readily available? Why is it that there aren't TV shows or forums dedicated to the advancement of our connection with the divine? When I had the privilege to die while living this past year and when brought back puzzle pieces of what is here and what is beyond came more into focus and what become even more clear is that most if not all are cautioned to not just give this information freely out. That is why in the matrix movies and other movies you may watch, they do not tell you that this is how reality is and this is how it works. They cannot because they will get killed or great harm could happen to them. Why? Because the energy of this reality wants to keep things a certain way, it wants to keep people dead mentally and spiritually while their physical bodies still can be used to construct the matrixes devices. And those that go against that, those that try to wake up the dead, are the adversary of our adversary alright. So, take heed in knowing that when people talk about certain things that we are going to talk about it doesn't come easy. It's been something that people have been contemplating quite a while before they try to do this. So, now we are going to get more into depth into the ego itself.

As I said previously the ego is what stops you in manifesting your ever creativity. You are an ever – creating being. You can create all types of things at any given time. Why? Because you have a mind and it's literally ever- creating. And so because we have been brainwashed by this reality to think things are a certain way. Because of that most people don't want to do the hard work that it takes or the time that it takes and it may not even be necessarily hard, but even so they do not want to take the time to put their ego in place. Now, why did I not say crush the ego? See crush is a very aggressive word; the things I am going to show you are putting your ego in place. But there are people here that want the quick way and they want to crush the ego. To give some examples about crushing the ego, in certain occultist orders because they want the quick route and of course this is the adversary's way of doing things, because it wants to do things more quickly to build the temples on the physical plane. So, if you were in their schools and you reached a high enough level even though you still have the ego because instead of showing humility, instead of helping your brothers here on this plane of existence, instead of doing that, which you were sent here for, what did they do? Of course they got fancy car and they feel because they have this fancy car, because they have material possession, they feel they are better than you, and some aren't even human anymore half the time (spirit displacement). All of us have met these people many times. So what do they do to crush the ego? A man would have sex with a man and because of this and especially and particularly if he's not homosexual, that literally belittles him. Because he has had sex with a man, so because of this it crushes his ego. But there are woman who are in the mystery schools too. Yes there are. And what do woman do to crush their egos in these mystery schools for quick results. Well the woman would have sex with an animal, but of course the results in the greater sense are false, it's not real.

It's something to pretty much put a band–aid over what's really there. So, of course it leads to suffering later on. These people in usually become very bitter later on in life. So, now I'm going to get into a very simple thing that I would like my listeners to do. Everyone who is listening, even if you are not listening live, if you get this recording after the fact, you can still partake in the exercise that I am about to explain shortly. Now as I mentioned many of you that are listening are indigo children, are considered what is called crystal children or star seeds or whatever term you want to say about it. It pretty much means you are special and you have a purpose. And why am I so adamant about saying that? Because the world is at stake; during all times in this reality, beings are sent into this reality to keep the balance, to keep things moving in a certain way. There is nothing wrong with if you were sent here and you're just one of the dead who works his job day in and day out, nothing is wrong with that and it is what it is.

But many of you were sent here for a divine purpose, to change things in this reality for the better or the worse. Some of you are actually agents for the other side that were sent here also for a purpose and I hope that I'm able to initialize this purpose and get you to live it out so we can move on to greater lessons later, maybe even together.

You have to do this lesson first to properly proceed through the next lesson. Before I actually get into this which is simple, I would like you to really understand the magnitude of this. For those of you who want to partake in these mysteries I would like for to not only do or practice what lesson 1 objectives is, but I also would like you to tell me what happened when you did what I'm asking you to do before you move on to lesson 2.

Exercise for Lesson 1

What I would like you to do is think in your mind, about a time in your past that you have done someone wrong. What I would like you to do is take the time to think about everyone you have hurt in the past whether it is a family member, or a friend or someone you really hurt for no reason, or someone you did some kind of atrocity to. It doesn't matter. Once you figure out who that person is, I would like you to get in contact with that person and tell that person you are sorry and tell them why you are sorry. Don't use language that puts the blame back on them. A lot of times, people that are egotistical or who are prideful, they will call you and tell you they are sorry but in the middle of the conversation, they revert the blame back to you saying "you shouldn't have done that and I wouldn't have done this." You are blaming them. And if you do this, you still have much more to learn about "The Outward Projection of the Ego" because you haven't learned that you're still egotistical.

This lesson here seems simple. How could me calling somebody I did something wrong to that I don't want to speak to at all really put my ego in check? Well those who may have even tried to do something like this in their past would understand. So just try it. The moment you think about that person, it brings up feelings of hate, feelings of anger, and feelings of resentment. Let's say you had a parent that literally did you wrong. I mean of course yes it's really their fault for treating you wrong, you were a child. It's really their fault, no doubt 100% about it, but during the course of them treating you wrong you may have harmed them, you may have literally cursed them out or anything. I'm not saying you were rightfully so for doing such, but that what you may have done. And as you look at it from the adult perspective from the I'm trying to master myself perspective you really shouldn't have done that, if you feel that way. Call them up. Call them up and let them know.

That is your lesson for the week. I would like to hear your comments and questions concerning it, let me know your stories of what you have done, your emotions you felt, etcetera. And we can move on from that point.

Lesson 2

Forgiveness of Self

The lesson today is about forgiveness of self. From Sunday to a few moments ago, we have over 1700 people that have tuned in to the radiocast. I didn't think it would be actually that popular. I appreciate all of you. I hope that many of you did do the lesson over the week. I hope you do have testimonials and or positive results to give to others. And so without further ado, I would like to start off the show by asking a question.

The question is what is the greatest expression one can give in their life to another?

I want you to think about this? What is the greatest expression one can give in their lifetime to another? Give you a second or two to think about it.

The greatest expression would be love.

Love is the greatest expression that you can give to yourself, to another, to the universe. And that is the most feared expression. Anger is not feared and sorrow is not feared. It is love. Pure love is the most flavorful delight. At this moment I want you to put everything aside. Because you are the most loved creature in your universe and the world has been contemplating destroying herself but she will not because of the love of you. So you are telling me that the world is pretty much or those who may be governors of this world are thinking about internally wiping humanity out because of the atrocities that people do to another. Yes. It is contemplated all the time, but it will not happen at least at this time, because of you.

So we are going to start off by re- capping lesson 1, which was the outward projection of the ego. Of course we stated that ego is a form of pride. In today's popular culture this would be rap music. Rap music today is very prideful. And that's also stemming from America. America is very prideful as she goes around the world destroying nations and entering into affairs that have nothing to do with her at all. Another example of pride would be the way that the United States goes around and of course bombing and tormenting all over the world vs. being the humble one, leading by example. Ego is the main culprit blocking your divine manifestations to take place. And of course ego is pride, pretty much between the first lesson and this lesson that you're about to hear today, these are the most important lessons, because without contemplating lesson one and contemplating lesson two your further manifestations after this point and further lessons as we do direct things concerning will as I train you in a way to go out and do specific things that will literally empower your will, you are pretty much going to waste your time, you're not going to get the full results that you would get if you complete lesson one and two.

We got into the actual nature of Smiths in the Matrix, how they were representatives of the force which is your adversary. But if you are the adversary that means I'm inherently yours. Lesson one's assignment was to apologize to someone you have done wrong to in one way or another during the course of your life. Now of course the best way to apologize to this person is either over the phone or in person. I hope all of you that are listening, who have listened to last week's show, did partake in the lesson because it will lead to manifesting abilities of will later on, If you have not listened, please do so soon. If you did listen and did the lesson please tell others about your experience comments questions during the Q and A tonight. All of these lessons deal with your will power.

The Buddha states:

In a controversy the instant we feel anger we have already ceased striving for the truth, and have begun striving for ourselves.

Forgiving yourself is probably one of the hardest things you will ever do in your life. Now as we go through lessons here tonight, some of you after you hear the exercises you will do during the week will go through it with no issue at all. But others will struggle with it. Do not be down because you struggle with it. But to forgive yourself for a wrong, for being so stupid, so arrogant in your wrong doing, to forgive yourself for you not being perceived as perfect. Even though there is no such thing as perfection and perfection is in the eye of the beholder, everything is in an ever state of perfection. So, I am going to say that one more time. Forgiving one's self for not being perceived as perfect, even though there is no such thing as perfection. Everything is ever perfecting.

It would be such a boring world of course if we came into this world all perfect. There is nothing to do, and then we all would be

11

just walking around, like hmm, the building is perfect, the lawn is perfect, the trees are perfect, and everything is perfect, so pretty much what is the point of existing. So, you're pretty much getting to the point of as the universe's time frame progresses. As you progress in your life, the whole point is to do self examination every day. Examine yourself; examine conversations that you had throughout the day. Reflect at the end of each night, reflect on self. Was I the best I could have been today? Did I work as well as I could have today? Did I think as well as I was supposed to have thought today? And as you think about these things on a daily basis you are perfecting yourself. And in perfecting yourself you are increasing your will.

Let's talk about magic, even though this wasn't my next thought but, I'm about to say this. Is there such a thing as real magic? Well I seen people use magic wands, I seen people use water, throwing it on to demons or whatever it maybe. I see people doing all these things externally but really what it is are just external expressions of their internal will. Are there real magic spells? Yes there are real magic spells. But most magic spells are just focusing your will. That's what all these lessons are about.

Now also forgive yourself for not wanting to be yourself. Forgive yourself for not wanting to be yourself, for wishing you were someone else or wishing you had their life. How many of us suffer from that? For giving yourself for not being in a way the Creator or your God would be proud of and humanity would praise. Men forgive yourself for the disrespect of our most precious resource, the woman. Women forgive the looking down and belittlement of the man, your protector. We all need each other to be.

Pastors, Imams, Metaphysicians get into aspects or vague definitions of living in your heart. But its like what really does that mean? They say it very vaguely. And when you ask them direct questions about any of these things, they go around it and at it and at the end you feel like you're still at the beginning. You feel like nothing has occurred. Now they say these things for two reasons. They say things like live in your heart, treat others as you would treat yourself because either one, they don't know the workings of the way or two they don't want you to know the inner workings of the way. It's either one or the other. They don't know or they don't want you to know. There is no inbetween. Let me also add this. This was not in my notes either. The adversary or lets call it the demon, if I'm the ying, lets call it the yang, the one that goes around causing havoc, etcetera. The one thing that this entity did is a very simple thing right. It caused no fuss and that has literally put humanity on its knees. What did this energy do? It put into the mind that there is no such thing as truth. The entity came up with opinions, so there is no such thing as right or wrong anymore. That is only your opinion. And so because they added just that simple thing, a person could come to you speaking the divine truth and you will say well that's your opinion. So you go through life thinking that everything is just an opinion.

Well there are truths and there are falsehoods. So, now we are going to do an exercise that deals with your heart. Now what I would like everyone to do, everyone who is listening on the line, everyone who is listening to this in the chat room, everyone who is on the internet, and all the other stations and all the other websites that this blog talk episode broadcasts from. What I would like to do, everyone close your eyes. Now that your eyes are closed I want you to picture your heart however you choose. Just picture your heart. The heart that is beating inside of your body, picture it in your mind. Now that you have that picture in your mind at this point I would like you to find and or create a comfortable place in your heart. It could be a room, it could be a beach, it could be a chair, it could be the floor or whatever. Whatever you decide picture this very place in your heart. Now that your eyes are closed now that you have utilized your heart, now that you have created a comfortable space in your heart, I want you to picture yourself there now. Picture yourself on that comfortable place in your heart. Now I would like you to take a deep breath through your nose. Breathe in as much as you can and breathe out slowly. Now you're in your heart, you took a deep breath and your relaxing in your heart and now speak from it. This is what is meant by living from your heart and what others mean by speaking from your heart. So, everyday you go out you want to speak from your heart, everyday. So, if you speak from your heart, unless your heart is darkened which evil thoughts conspire within your heart, if you actually live within your heart the world would be in peace and that's what the adversary does not want you to know.

Is it difficult to live in your heart? Yes, if you have never done it. Yes it is very difficult. But each day, when you wake up in the morning you visualize yourself in your heart on that relaxing place. When someone comes to you in a confrontational way, when someone comes to you starting an argument for no reason, or even if you get upset for no reason, you have to remind yourself that you're inside your heart and the heart cannot take certain vibrations and certain frequencies of thought.

I have a few quotes from a few different books concerning the heart. The heart is the most important thing you have. Through your heart love is expressed to the world. If you did not have a heart, the world would be heartless. The world is getting to that point as we speak. People are so cruel to one another. So now what does the bible say about the heart?

Proverbs 4:23:

Keep your heart with all vigilance for from it springs the flow of life.

Psalms 51 and 10

Create a clean heart in me,
oh God and renew a right spirit in me, oh God.

Proverb 23:26

For where your treasure is there will your heart be also.

Interesting, interesting. Now that's what the bible says about the heart. Now what does the Quran say about the heart?

Al Baquar 2:283

Do not conceal the testimony.
Whoever conceals it in his heart is sinning.

Why? Because of pride and ego, even shame. If something fantastic has happened to you, express it. If you did lesson one and you felt something that you never felt before, express it. Even if no one wants to hear, believe me, I want to hear and I enjoy hearing your testimonial.

Al Ahzab 64:11
Whoever believes in Allah, Allah gives his heart.

Al Azerk 33:4
Allah has not made for any man two hearts in his chest.

Now what does that mean? It means that there are no contra-dictory actions of the heart. The heart cannot contradict itself. So, if you're doing evil actions, if you spoke things about a person you shouldn't have spoke, that was your heart and there was no denying that to try to speak your way out of that. That was an expression of your heart. So, in the Quran, Allah has not given two hearts. Ok, now what does Buddhism or Buddhists says about the heart?

Nahla hama pata chapter 6 verse 50
Once man finds no peace, neither enjoys the pleasure nor delight nor goes to sleep or feels secure while the dark or hatred is stuck in the heart.

So your thoughts thinking about things warps your mind, but it also messes with your heart. It makes your heart hurt. Let's say your today's rap which is some of the harshest music along with death metal and stuff like that and you go around a grandmother one who is full of love and you played that type of music, they will say "oh child that hurts my heart." And of course that's because many of us were not taught the understandings of these things, were not taught the ways of the heart, were like what does grandma mean, what is she talking about? Well if you were living in your heart, listening to that type of music, listening to someone pride fully speak about the way they will kill your whole family for ten dollars or some crack or some crap like that. That really does hurt the heart and you know you have been living in your heart for a long time when things like that start to hurt it like when people who act crazy on the street start to hurt your heart, when you listen to lies by politicians and you know that these lies will hurt the people that will hurt your heart. What else does Buddhism or the Buddha say?

Better than a thousand hollow words is one word that brings you peace.

Someone spoke for twenty hours about all kinds of stuff and you left and you felt exactly the same way you came. What else is said by the Buddha?

Thousands of candles can be lighted from a single candle and the life of that candle shall never be shortened.

Happiness never decreases by being shared. How deep is that and how simple is that? You can be the light to the world. Now you do these exercises and your will become more powerful, bring happiness into the world, don't bring more shame, more despair, more anger. And that happiness that you bring will bring peace. Believe me in hearing all of your testimonials and hearing what happened when you expressed yourself from lesson 1, it brought happiness to me. Just to hear the happiness that you felt from going through your journey.

Also, the Buddha says

The way is not in the sky, it is in the heart.

So, externally people are looking up to the sky or down to the earth. But all the answers are in your heart. As you live in your heart more as that place in your heart becomes more flourished you will notice yourself.

Now, what did Martin Luther King Jr. say about the heart?

Once said, we have two choices, to peacefully coexist or to destroy ourselves. Each and every day we ourselves encounter and generate prejudice attitudes and behaviors. If we are to ultimately survive on this tiny planet called our home, we are to learn to appreciate and value each other as human beings and live together in peace. While a general disarmament of all nation states would seem ideal, this process cannot be done till we have first disarmed our own individual hearts.

16

The heart must be very important, that pretty much everyone in history that is a prominent person speaks about the heart. That is interesting that through the heart is your way to happiness. Allow me to add this into it. Now of course these females on the line may be able to chime into this and some of the males may have heard this. Now you hear this more from females than males. Males will express their heart, but many times from what I have heard and observed, many times a female who has been hurt in her past, genuinely hurt, now when the next guy comes along he is a great guy and he is very nice to this woman. And of course a nice guy maybe likes to hear that he is loved also. Who doesn't like to hear that they are loved and appreciated? But she will not express this because she doesn't want her heart to hurt. So pretty much she put up a fortress around her heart that nothing could get out. But guess what? Nothing could get in either. It goes both ways. So, no expressions will go out of her heart no expressions will come in her heart. Because even if that male expressed to her deeply I love you, or I care for you, or I won't hurt you it will not be able to penetrate. Now this is the time of change by expressing love which is better known as the Creators vibration. The whole reason for existence is for an expression of love. What other expression could create existence? Does the expression of anger create existence? No. Does the expression of sorrow, the expression of despair create this whole reality that we live in? No, not at all. It was the expression of love.

They say change the world by changing yourself, without giving instructions. This is false misdirection. We're getting into real change that can change the world by changing the state of the heart. We must change the world together. I am very strong spiritually of course and carry the souls of many sons with me and believe me that I'll be by your side right foot forward in this grand act. Now lesson 3's exercise will be in three parts and this lesson will be a lot more difficult than your past lessons. Now each of these lessons, let me reiterate the point that everything you are hearing that everything that you are learning is to literally empower your will, empower your will for anything you want to do in general, as long as it doesn't affect someone else. Empower your will to make direct sustainable observable change in your life and also the world. Now of course most of the world is lost it seems, most of the world doesn't know about Chem- trails, most of the world doesn't know about or observe that this world is going to the dumps pretty fast. So, who is to change it?

17

Obviously those who come out and say we just all need to get along? That's a false misdirection. That in general is impossible. That in general at this time is not going to happen. Because of that it takes those who are spiritually gifted who have the inkling to change the world. First by changing your heart.

Exercise 2

Now the lesson for this week is in three parts. First upon waking each morning I want you to verbally express love for life and the opportunity for living it to your creator and to yourself. That's the first thing I want you to do every day of this week.

Lesson two when living each day I only want to speak from that comfortable place in your heart. So not only in the morning are you expressing your love for life to your creator and yourself, by each day from that point on your going to speak from that comfortable place in your heart, everyday.

Now the third one is going to be a slight working on your will. For this week, I would like to find one person whose heart is suffering. This could be a homeless person, it could be a crying child, or whoever you may come upon that fits this. I want you to express to them the love of your heart for them and the love life has in your own way for them. Do, I want you to say specific words to them? No I want you to say whatever is in your heart. So, instead of walking past that person seeing their suffering a lot, you don't have to spend an hour with them, you don't have t o spend more than five minutes with them. Just spend a moment of your time to express love, so that they know the world still does love them that they know the Creator is shining through them and that the Creator is shining through you loves them.

And you would be surprised what that does to someone's life. Don't be afraid if you stumble. Don't be afraid if you stutter, just express what purely comes from your heart. So, as always just in lesson 1, I don't waste a lot of time I get directly to the point. I try to give you the most pertinent information, the most powerful information I hope that you did receive it and hope you are able to use it to empower your life.

Lesson 3

Guarding of the Mind, Nothingness is the Way

You are nothing and your existence is nothing. There is no racism, no hatred, no bigotry, or no I. There is no I. There is no such thing as the I. There is only us. Why even try to rationalize nothing into something. This would be equivalent to insanity. How is your life at the moment? Do you feel it could be better, what about worse? So throughout day, why not think about such things and enjoy your present. Enjoy the moment in existence. Existence as the present needs your attention. As you build your present your future will be secured, so there is no need to think about it or worry.

You are an instrument and as such can be tuned in or tuned out and can even be tuned out past the point of normal coherent frequencies. Everything has a frequency, even a rock. Existence is sound. Sound is frequency. Frequency is vibration. Vibrations being in a state of ever changing can be manipulated or distorted. Distortions come from internal or external influences. Influences could be a rock, a person, or your mind. The higher you vibrate the more fluid you are in a space. Think of it like air. Air is moving of vibration of thoughts in the mind. Since we are on the subject of vibrations, let us get into a subject of grand significance it concerns soul transfers or a better name is semi – permanent frequency transfers. It even more importantly concerns humanity's most important resource, the woman.

Now in general, the makeup of men is a projectile energy inherent. That would mean that women in their makeup are a vacuum of energy inherent. It does not mean a woman sucks the energy from a person, it doesn't mean that a woman is a bad thing, 100% not at all, it is just inherently that this is the nature of the makeup. When a man and a woman come together she consumes his essence. This can be a good or a bad thing based on the circumstances. This essence or vibration better known as frequency instantly brings her essence up or down. But more importantly this bonds the man's essence with her semi – permanently for life. Now a days this is a more permanent act and it is only a permanent act because people have not been taught the right ways of this reality. Because we are getting into the act of child birth, many of you have been talking about how to bring forth a God. A spirit that is high enough and can literally change the world with a thought. Well this will get to certain understandings why some issues with that and if you haven't done that yet how you possibly can do that. If certain mistakes have happened in your life willingly or unwillingly people have not been taught how to discharge that out of your essence. So, now instead of it being a semi – permanent act it is now a permanent act.

21

What could happen from this transfer that happens each and every time a woman and a man get together, the positive the woman takes on a stronger personality type that increases her vibration, if children come from this union, the children will have certain personality and vibration traits that would help them in many circumstances that they wouldn't have otherwise. There are certain essences that come from man and there are certain essences that come from a woman. Now the not so positive, the woman takes on a lower personality type. This leads to certain mental disorders. Children that come from this type of union may not be mentally and spiritually equipped from the start. Now whether it's from positive interactions or not so positive interactions, multiple frequencies and essences or vibrations lead to over activity.

Meaning the men inside your mind argue, they fight and sometimes they play against your well being.

Part of the essence of that man is in her mind and the distortions that are thought about on a daily basis such as not being able to focus 100% come from that partially. This leads to a woman having several personality types, one minute she's acting like Man A and an hour later she is acting like Man B. It eventually leads to bitterness, selfishness, ego and a permanent delusion of the world. Now why am I focusing on the woman? I could have started off these few statements concerning men. But you raise the children. And of course the father's role is to raise his son or daughter also. Yes, we know that and we know the seed that is planted into the earth comes from the man, yes we know that. But in general, a first step of a child's life is to be with the mother, to bond with the mother. You're teaching the child something a man could only dream to teach. So, that's why it's so important.

Children who are brought forth from this type of situation typically are confused and just do not get it no matter who tells them what. So you have a child and you are in this type of vibration, frequency that we are speaking of, no matter what you tell that child, how much perfect sense you make, the child does not understand. It doesn't mean your child is dumb at all or anything like that. But it has to be handled a specific way. Now how can they not be confused, its multiple mind sets dwelling within. Which mind set will win, only time will tell? Only way to get through to them is if you come to them in multidimensionality since they are multiple vibrations you

22

are dealing with within this child. You have to come at them in a multifaceted way at first, not coming at them this way this minute, the next minute you do it this way, the third minute you do it that way, etcetera. No your doing each thing separately. You have to come at them totally multiple ways at the same time.

Now we are going to move on to the vibrations of magic, real magic. Is there such thing as real magic? Yes. Harry Potter magic, no. But the effect is devastating used the wrong way. This reality has pulled a cloak over your head to not allow certain knowledge into your mind to block you from the obvious that is all around you. They tell you there is no such thing as certain topics at school, at home, or even at church mosques, the temple, when literally this entire existence is a magical note.

The singing, tone, frequency or vibration thought of reality.

Some examples of modern day magic are rotational pull of the moon and stars. They say that it is gravity, but it is invisible. So, an invisible force is doing this. This is known as magic. No matter what name you may want to call it, someone or something, some would say the creator of life. Still this thing this unseen unknown thing is magic in nature. What else is magical in nature? How a TV works, a listener would say now; "Well I could explain to you Priest Amen right here how a TV works. A frequency comes from the station, it travels through your wires at home, and your TV itself through a complicated process shoots out millions of lights/beams at the screen, which in turn gives you a picture." What you just explained was a process. It wasn't how it works. No one can explain how it works. Now the creator of that or the one who brought that type of magic here who got it from the other side, they could probably explain to you how it works, the kind of instruments they use. But no one else can because it's not meant for you to know. Because if you knew that would start you creating all types of things and you would start to bring this reality more in balance or bring the reality more out of balance based on your thoughts and actions.

There are different types of magic, but we are going to start very basic, very low level, but powerful. The magic of stones, crystals, gems. There are reasons why certain gems and stones cost into the millions. But in general I'm just giving more terms for what is commonly known as a rock. Now for those who play video games, we are not talking about those whom just play sport games, we are talking about the people (male or female) that play magic based games. Games that throughout the game you get rings, chains, amulets, and all these types of magical based games. If you notice in these types of games for those that don't know these types of games, I'm going to explain. You start off the game bare, you have nothing and throughout the game you may see on the ground a ring and you pick up this ring and the ring may be of amethyst or sapphire or citrine, whatever the ring may be. And this ring will boost your ability and pretty much since you found it; it may not be that much of value. But let's say your intelligence just for arguments sake is zero or your intelligence is so little that pretty much there is none. All of a sudden when you put this ring on your intelligence is plus one. And as you go up throughout the game, as you become more advanced in the game you could buy more jewelry more amulets, rings and stones and armor and so forth. Sometimes, in the game you may put on a ring that will boost your intelligence to 500. So you went from 0 to 500 just by putting on this one ring. Of course they give you slots for multiple rings or multiple chains or whatever. That's how magic based games work for all systems. Well they are trying to tell you something. A lot of ancient indigenous cultures of this planet, all over the world and the ones that come from elsewhere typically plate themselves in all types of amulets, silver, and gold. There is also a reason for that. They are not just doing it to say; hey I'm the biggest guy on the block. Its magic involved in that. So certain amulets, gems, and crystals will boost certain aspects of your persona to a certain degree. Some will say this is not true. I will rebuttal by saying why is there quartz crystals and other metals in pagers, mainframes, and servers around the world. If you take it out, it shuts down and it doesn't work. Or if you stand by certain radioactive rocks, this invisible energy will kill you, or if you ingest certain rocks like lead, it will do the same.

It must be more significance into gemstone and rocks than what you believe. For example, let's talk about amethyst. It has many attributes, but a few help to promote dreams, psychic abilities, if you have it on you, it can promote peace and love within oneself. Also, if you put it under your pillow at night time, it's known to ward off insomnia and nightmares. Does this happen instantaneously? No. That's Harry Potter magic. In this reality things take time. So, if you go get an amethyst stone or a pendant, whatever it may be you will want to wear it all the time until you get the benefits. Now some would say you should wear it this day of the week because it's more in line with

Venus, Mars or Jupiter. Now you're making this simple subject again complicated. Do what vibrates to you, what seem to pull you in. But before we get to that momentarily, we also have plants, fruits, and herbs that also have a magic vibration. When you make the perfect smoothie in the morning, you are actually utilizing chemistry and a bit of alchemy. And you're also utilizing magic because you know what goes together. And the benefit of all of that is now you have an appetizing treat. See this reality purposely or those who are in control purposely want to make everything super complicated, so super interlaced, so super this or that so you cannot figure out how simple things actually are, it is a bit of mind based compartmentalization.

The vibrations of herbs can help heal you. The vibrations of dance can help or heal you, also the places that you visit. There are places on this earth that are geared toward helping and healing you based on the helping and healing you need at that time. With the advent of the internet, you are tuning into this show in the Chicago area. Obviously many calls are coming in from all over the world tuning in at this time is to help you with the healing you need. Obviously you wouldn't have stumbled upon it. Everything happens for a reason, regardless if it is accepted or not. Not more importantly than all of the above is just to tell you lastly to guard your mind.

Exercise 3

Well let me get into the lesson for you to do this week. The lesson for this week comes in two parts.

First you are going to become a researcher. I want you to utilize books, the internet, whatever you have to do. I want you to find a stone, crystal, rock to help facilitate your need. The internet of course is a great research tool. And most stones can be found in your local area f or a few dollars. Most stones are not that expensive at all. I want you to find one for what I want find one for whatever purpose you feel internally. Find a stone based on your need, that you need at this time and just carry it around with you every day. That's it.

The second part of the lesson is to guard your mind. I don't want you to watch TV, listen to the radio in the car. No turning on the TV when you walk into the house just for the sake of turning on the TV. No needless internet browsing. Everyone loves to get on the internet and we will waste 8 hours on the internet and now it's the next day. I want you to in all that silence, it's going to come a time when you're not going to know how to deal with yourself. You're going to be like man I'm tired of listening to and being myself, I want to be consumed by something, I want to something to consume me. I want to watch person of interest or the wire, or the walking dead which is a pretty good show. I want to watch that. It came on a few hours ago. I want to watch the re- run tomorrow. No, I don't want you watching anything, especially something like that. I want you to meditate within your-self. When you're in the car driving I want you to listen to your own thoughts. You'll be able to listen to how good your thoughts are or how negative they may actually be. I just want you to observe them. In the observation of your own thoughts you're able to facilitate your own prescription for yourself to get yourself to get yourself in order.

You're going to start to affect your environment. What do you mean effect your environment? You mean use magic? Yes, by the right use of your will. Aww come on, you're fooling, and that's not possible. Some people create negative environments around them ev-ery day by the use of magic. Your mind is doing it. But you also can use your mind to create positive actions in your life every day. Things come out the blue like here take this. Like what, I didn't ask for this. You just need to hold it, you can have it. Here I'm leaving. It's like what? And that's just what you need. You would be surprised. Expect unexpected things to happen, whether they are good or bad. Expect the unexpected. Find out who you are internally by thoughts that tend to walk past and stick around. Some people project themselves as being this person or being that person, but as you sit in silence this week for one solid week, but I suggest you do it more. These lessons are lifelong lessons.

Lesson 4

A Use of Will:
Utilizing your will to affect
change in your environment

I'm going to start off with a statement by Bohdi Sanders, he stated that warriors confront the evil that most people refuse to acknowledge. That's a deep statement in itself. It's not that they don't know about it, they just refuse to acknowledge its existence. Because if they acknowledge its exists, that means that they have to do something about it, and if they don't do something about it that means that they are held spiritually accountable. So that is what you see in life today, whether it's CEOs of companies or whether it be your mother or father. When you come to them with the truth, and it makes perfect sense, you got to understand this and they act like they don't want to acknowledge it. You know they understand. How can they not understand? Because they know if they acknowledge certain truths that holds them spiritually accountable. So they play a role of ignorance. As they say ignorance is bliss. The meaning of love without ownership is just that. In parts of the world, especially where ego and pride dwell men especially like to feel they own a woman, like how they own a car. Now this also goes for woman especially in this new age. But the fact is that no matter how much you love someone it does not mean you own anything of them, not even a follicle of their hair do you own. The need to own something spawns from deep insecurities from within. It's just like when people copyright or patent something that they supposedly came up with. Did you own that thought or does the Creator own it? And if the Creator owns that thought, wasn't that thought given to better your life, but more than likely the lives of the world. If you do not own your own thoughts, how can you own anything that comes forth from them.

Why it is the threat of death makes people a lot more aware of their lives. Because they understand that their life is totally out of their hands, but even more so many people either now want to live their lives because they might not have another chance for them to do so. They came to that realization or even more so they feel like it might be a judge over their actions in life and they want to get in good kudos before time is up. You see that a lot of times when people hit the age of 50 or so, half of their life is gone all of a sudden sometimes they act totally different, they get holier than thou. Or they become the world's nightmare. Now tonight we are going to get deeper into the esoteric and the occult. ou all are the evil ones. I'm tired of this, I just have to come out and say it.

You all who are listening on the chat lines, on the live line, all over radio land, on the internet, you all are the evil ones. Yes, all of you! You are the evil ones. You are the ones going against this reality. Doomed for Hell. Now of course some of you are laughing and some of you are like what the heck. Some of you are like Priest Amen you have finally did it, you have been between realities for too long. You have gone mad man. Well not quite, not quite mad. But you are the evil ones. This is factual. But not in the perspective you may think. If you may follow me on a journey through the mind's eye. Evil or what we call evil, the agreed upon evil doesn't ever call itself evil if you notice. Evil doesn't call itself evil. It never has. And it probably never will. That's the first thing. The second thing evil is always on point. It's always on point moving ever toward its goal. If you notice one thing about evil, it's moving man. Day, night, wake, or sleep twenty four hours a day, seven days a week and 365 days a year it's moving toward a goal. Evil just wants to go along its path and spread let's say, for lack of a better word. It just wants to move along and it wants you to join it. But the thing about it is that, it wants you to join by your own free will. I'm talking about real evil, the energy of evil. The energy of evil never requests that you join. Never. You have to join the evil willingly in your heart. Now all of this is what evil does. Now everything I have mentioned thus far was what the supposed evil does. In general, the statements itself are not evil. First the evil never calls itself evil. Second evil is ever – moving toward its goal. Shouldn't everyone be moving towards their goals? So that's not evil either. And evil just wants to do what it does. It just wants to spread and continue to move forward. That's what evil wants to do. There is nothing wrong with any of these three statements, 100% nothing wrong. The fact is if most people did those three statements, the world may not be the way it is currently is. But let's move on. Now all of this and the above I just mentioned, that's what evil does.

But you are the one who spreads the lies. What? When is the last time you told a lie to your neighbor, yourself. Evil actually doesn't do that. Evil just moves on the go. Like I said we are not talking about low level gang–banging, racial prejudice and all that low level nit-gritty, not worthy to sit at the table type of evil. We are going deeper than that. Now, you are the one that can't seem to get the energy to get up and get going in the morning just to move forward in your own life. Why don't you want to live life? It's not the point of being here in this existence, to live life. I thought that was the

30

point. To enjoy life, but when you came out your dream state, the only thing you want to do is go back to your dream state. You do not want to live life. You want to live dead. You want to be in the spiritual realm.

Remember I start off this statement by saying you are the evil ones. You are the one who wants someone to feel sorry for you. People walk around with their head down and they want people to feel sorry for them. That's evil. The action in itself is evil. Evil doesn't walk around wanting anyone to feel sorry for it. It will sacrifice itself at the drop of a dime to do whatever it needs to do. But you won't sacrifice a hair follicle. And even though you wouldn't sacrifice a hair follicle, you want people to feel sorry for you. People say aww, can I help you out? Can I make life easy for you? When you have not lifted a dime, you have not caused one drop of sweat. So you see I'm trying to paint a picture here. So if you're really looking at evil for what it is, it seems like good in a way. Because if you truly did that within your life, it would be even better. But the thing about supposed evil spreading is that it doesn't force you to move out of the country and move to the big cities with flashy lights. It just puts up flashy lights. You are the one who came to the city and decided to enjoy its spoiled flesh. Cities in general are places where negative energy dwells and summons or seems to call those spirits on the physical plain who prefer to dwell in its belly. That is why some of the strangest people that tend to abort all local customs tend to dwell in the downtown areas of major cities.

Some of you are from the country. It was nice, you had a farm, and you had fresh fruit and vegetables. You had good water. Life could be considered slow if you compare it to the life of the cities. But it was a good life. And so because you turned on the TV and see the flashy lights of the city, it lured you to the city. And so now you want to dwell in caves known as apartments or you stay in houses that are very close and congested with the next neighbor, the air is of poor quality, the food is of poor quality. Now some would say that cities are evil, they are so evil. But the evil energy of the city did not force you to come to the city. It just put up flashy lights. That's all it did. That's like saying I put up a flashy light and it caused all of you to murder someone. That's foolishness. Don't you have more control over yourself than light? The evil doesn't force you to participate in porn on the internet. Yes it is there. We

31

all know that porn is on the internet. But isn't it up to you to type in the coordinates to get there. So, it seems more than not, you're the evil one, but we are going to continue on. Evil it doesn't force you to commit any form of crime; it just leads you the way. It is up to you to walk the path. So, again just because it's a street heading straight to disaster and there is a street sign that says disaster, you don't have to walk down that street. That's factual. I mean you don't. All people of sound mind can agree on that. But instead you walk down that street anyway. And then when disaster happens you say it's evil. I got requests to go a little bit deeper. So, why call evil, evil. So evil for making the abortion clinic or are you the evil one for partaking in it. So making up a thousand and one excuses about why you have to go there. So of course people blow up abortion clinics and so forth and say their evil. Just think about this, an abortion clinic is just a brick building. It may go under certain that lead you to think that it's one thing when in actual reality it is something totally different. But still you go to this brick building and you had to open the door, you had to walk in, you had to sign the forms. You had to do that, you had to lie on the table, because you can sign a form and say skip this I'm not doing this and leave. But you sat on the table. So, who is the evil one, the building, just because they put up a building or you for partaking in the act? This lesson if anything else is showing how one should be responsible for their actions. Now so far what I said about evil is that it really seems that what is really evil is you, and what we call "evil" the energy, the force is showing you what your true nature is.

Those who look at the surface of things would say yes all of those things that you mentioned are evil. But when you give things a little bit more critical thought, there is nothing in the general statements that is evil in itself. The abortion clinic isn't evil, no, it's just a building and that is what they want to do inside of that building. But they need your willingness for them to do it. If you don't do it, it doesn't happen.

It's literally as simple as that.

You need to comply. You have to comply. So if you don't comply this doesn't happen. So, really when you give things a little more critical thought, there is nothing evil, if you get what I am saying. Let me continue on. So is it the supposed evil, just trying to show your true nature? Is what you call evil just trying to show you who you truly are? To show you who you really are, to show you who you are running from., to show you who you are scared to be? Priest Amen it sounds like you are calling me Satan, because I partake in everything you just mentioned. Hey I'm not saying anything. I'm just making a statement. Is evil trying to show you who you are, who you have been running away from your entire life?

You call out this energy as evil, which hasn't done anything evil as of yet. A listener stated in chat that he or she knows something that is 100% evil. So what is it? "It's the military, the military is definitely evil." How is machinery evil? "A gun is evil." No it is not! It's just a machine that if pointed or looks in a certain direction and has a purpose, yes. But it's not evil. Well what did you do with the gun? "I picked up that gun and I shot somebody." Well you are the evil one, not the gun. What's the military? The military is a conglomerate of people that drive machines that destroy people. So is it the machine that is evil or is it the person driving the machine that's evil

So what do you do once you come upon these situations, those who are brave enough call out this energy and say its evil and that is should change. Isn't that an evil act? You go to these abortion clinics and say doctor you are evil with force if necessary. But he is just standing there; no one had to partake in it at all. And he is just giving people his time. But you actually committed the evil act; you actually bust open the door and physically assaulted the Doctor stop doing abortions. So, who is the one who is evil? I'm just stating a question, not making a statement. Who is the one who is really evil? That's for you to really decide.

Now supposed evil doesn't go around saying who is evil and who is good, do you notice that? Evil never does that. But the ones who call themselves good, the ones that call themselves the righteous ones, point fingers all day, saying who is evil and who's good. Isn't that an evil act, to go around telling people whose evil and whose good? Telling people over here you are good and welcomed while telling people over there you're not welcome to come to my house, let the Lord cast you into hell. And isn't that an actual judgmental evil act? Is evil more disciplined within ego, in separation of self, while you wallow in the self I. Evil, does seem a lot more disciplined does it not? They don't go around doing certain things even on a global scale. When riots are going on, when all these protests are going on, the ones we call evil say let us give them a free speech zone. We want you to go over there because we want to feel safe. What does the supposed good say? No, we want to get next to you, we want to throw things at your building, we want to scare you, we want to kill you if we are able. What? Isn't that the evil act? So it does seem like evil is more disciplined or what we call evil. It seems a lot more disciplined in every aspect. Evil knows about the separation of self, while you wallow in the self I.

I this and I that. I need to this for self. Isn't that an evil act? So in Star wars the movie, every time the supposed evil was just walking along and wants to do what it does and spread, all of a sudden here comes the Jedi saying you can't go here, you can't go there, stay in your place! That's what the Jedi do. The Jedi goes around telling the supposed evil you can't do stuff. Isn't that the evil act? It just wants to do what it does. It's not forcing you to join; you decide to join because of the supposed benefits you can get. And so all of a sudden the Jedi doesn't like that too many people and planets for the Sith and moving toward the supposed dark side. Even the Jedi calling it the dark side is an evil connotation on people, places and things. And so when their walking along and the Jedi comes along saying you can't go here, you can't go there, stay in your place, the evil is like whoa man, I'm just walking along, it's not my fault others are joining me. They like the things that I do, they want o hear the things that I say. They join me. Then all of a sudden here come the supposed good guys telling people they can't join me and that I need to stay over here. I pretty much need to stay in my place. What? Isn't that an evil act?

Now in this world your neighbors they just want to believe in their Jesus, they just want to believe in their Allah that is all. And here comes you and what do you do? You step and say stop looking at those nefarious Gods who are really representations of something else, something more sinister. Here you go the next day saying telling about the Federal Reserve no more federal than the federal express. It is not an actual government entity! Government gave the power to print money to an entity whose notes don't mean anything. They are worthless and before you can pull out your notebook with constitutional, bill of rights and other fact based citations to back this claim, what do the people say? They say shut up and sit down. We don't want to hear it. What do the good call these people; they call them the ones that are sleeping while the good is supposedly the awakened. Now how evil is that statement. That's putting you over someone else. You're saying you're awakened, which means that other people must not be awakened. They must be sleep, in ignorance.

So your next move is to go for the Christians and their church stating the fact that even if the story was true, there was no Jesus. There was no J thousands of years ago. There was no J in the alphabet at that time. And in fact you have done diligent research and have found that the beginning of today's Christendom roots and in facts the beginning of the story of this savior called Jesus was conspired at the Council of Nicaea at approximately 321Ad. That's all they want to do is believe in their Jesus. You bust open the doors to their church and you start blabbing off saying these supposed facts from your supposed research. You're doing a dissertation as if your about to obtain your doctorate and you're not even in university! You say "Their worshipping Satan up there!" Remember you're coming into their church; they just wanted to worship their Jesus, that's it. Regardless what color, whether he was white, black, orange or yellow!

You bust open their church. And now they tell you to leave and that your tainted words need to go back to your master Beelzebub. That's what they tell you. So they're saying that you were spawned from Satan. That's what they tell you and their quoting from the bible scriptures, and you don't belong here and that literally you are the evil one.

Black is white and white is black. To move toward the light is really moving toward darkness and moving toward the darkness is really moving toward the light. The darkness is and is always flowing throughout this reality. The light is not the natural state of the universe. The supposed God in the Garden of Eden which is earth stated to you that "you will know not." So to mean, you will be ignorant that's what the God of this Earth, of Eden which is Earth said. You shall not know the workings of this reality. Now what does the supposed evil one do, Satan? He says hey, here are some books; they will give you the knowledge of self. I will be here to guide you through this world and the next. I will show you the one true way.

Moving along to some tips to heighten your senses. Close your eyes to enhance your hearing. So when you're watching TV close your eyes and listen to everything that goes on, now you want to focus totally at times on your mantra, which is your breath. So sometimes you want to sit back when it's quiet and just breathe. Focus on your senses, your hearing, your touch, focus on your breathing. While you eat something, close your eyes and focus on the taste, that's how you grow your palette. For example, when you taste something, close your eyes and focus on the taste. Certain tastes have a beginning taste, a medium taste, and they have an end taste. There is a beginning, middle, and end. When you taste certain foods, even an apple there are certain tastes that you taste right in the beginning but they disappear. There are certain tastes you taste, they are only in the end. Fried food is going to destroy your tastes, so you want to eat decent quality food.

Listen to wildlife, including plants. Go to the forest preserve. If you have a lot of plants in your house, just keep it quiet, don't put on any music or anything and just sit near them and just listen. You will just start to hear and feel thoughts that you know you didn't think of per say. When you smell you want to smell deeply, but if you're in the city and there is a busted pipe near youno you don't want to smell that. But if it's good food or a person male or female that smells good to you, take in the deep smells. Smell the different essences that are around you. You want to touch objects with your eyes closed. Explore the textures, vibrations, and temperatures of different objects. This is going to enhance your sense of touch. And lastly, feel the wind utilizing all your senses, go outside on a windy day and just feel the wind. The wind speaks to you also. What is wind? Wind is the thoughts or the vibrations of the one, the Creator. When you just sit back and you just listen and you feel the wind, all of a sudden all types of thoughts cross your mind. And even certain things will speak to you, because the wind is thought in motion.

Now there are herbs that develop psychic abilities. The first one is cinnamon. The second one is peppermint, the third one is star anise, and the fourth is sage. The fifth is rose, like the plant you know the flower rose. And the sixth one is honeysuckle. Now if you really want to enhance your third eye or open up your third eye, every morning when you wake up make some kind of tea. It doesn't matter what kind of tea. Say specifically green tea. There are two specific ingredients that you want to put in this green tea. One ingredient is cayenne pepper, the hottest cayenne pepper that you can find, put a few dabs in there to see how much you can handle. If you can handle a lot, then put a lot, if you can only handle a little bit and work yourself to a moderate amount of cayenne pepper in your tea. And then also what you want to put in your tea at the same time is ginger. So ginger and cayenne pepper and a drop of sage will not hurt. Of course you can add honey and a lemon to taste. It is as simple as that. If you do that every morning you will start to feel your third eye pulsate without you doing anything else.

Exercise 4

For the first week, I want you to find a closet in your house or your apartment. Somewhere which you can feel closed in and doesn't have direct air current and I want you to relax. Take a few deep breathes and as you breathe in deeply and exhale, I want you to try to externally sense the airflow around you. Before you did this, you made sure there is no airflow. And so you are going to try to sense the airflow around you. This will get you to feel the spirit of the world, the universe of the one. The more you seek out to feel this, you will feel it. It becomes a point where it is so activated because you have been working that muscle, that energy muscle, the feeling muscle, you will feel the earth. You will feel the presence of the universe. So every day this week starting from Monday to Sunday, specifically this one exercise only.

Then the following week, will need a partner. You will need help for this one. I want you to blindfold yourself and stand up straight and have your legs slightly ajar. And I want your partner; to slowly, very slowly point their finger out at you and try to touch you some-where on your body. And it's your job to sense where it's coming from. So you're sitting blindfolded and your eyes are closed, your legs are ajar, and your hands are to the side. And they can pick a random spot, each time they're just going to put their hand forward and try not to touch you somewhere. The first week you were sensing the energy around you, the energy of the universe, the second week the goal is to sense when someone breaks the energy field that surrounds you and all living things. Usually people are so weak that the bubble can be barely seen. It's less than a paper width seen against you, be-cause it's so weak. But with these exercises, you are going to increase it, so your energy may go literally go across a room. So, as they keep coming at you, your whole job is to hit their hand. So, as they are coming at you to try to touch your chest lets say, you will move their hand to block their hands away. As you do this week after week, you will be surprised what you sense.

Lesson 5

An Energy Ball:
Utilizing your inner will
for direct change

Being yourself is more powerful and more enlightening than you may think. Now some would say being myself is what got me into the predicament that I am in now. Being myself has ruined me financially. Being myself this and being myself that, I would rebuttal yet again and say what you call being yourself was you trying to dwell in the expectations that others have of you. Have you ever just actually been yourself? There was a meeting we had in the summer months and some individuals came to my home and we got into pretty much being yourself. And a person had mentioned that being their true self is one of violence let's say. They have a fiery heart and they tend to not want to hear the nonsense of others and if someone literally steps on their toes and betrays them they literally want to harm them. Now some other master teachers would say crush that fire and be not of the dark side and so and so forth. That is true. But then you are not being yourself, so that's a contradiction. Now I don't promote violence or anything like that. But what I am saying be yourself being your true divine self. Be literally the greatest self that you can be.

Now obviously in history there have been those who were themselves and we could commonly agree it wasn't for the benefit of humanity. And they have literally destroyed humanity, but they have been themselves. You can fault them for doing everything else, but one thing is you cannot fault them for not being themselves. But we can fault you for not being yourself. If you're not yourself literally everything that spawns from you is not a formulation of who you are. From where will you go to school at, the tea you drink, everything is not who you are so you have literally lived life not being you.

Allow me tell you a story, regardless if you believe this story is true or not and regardless if you believe that the Christian Jesus was a real person or not, that's not for debate. But in the story Jesus hung around the thieves, the whores, people who society has turned their back on. The ones people certainly do not want to be around in reality. And why did he hang around these people? Because they were real, they knew who they were and did not fake it. Tomorrow they may be something else, but now they are this and that is who they are. The whore knew she was a whore. She didn't hide it. She was a whore. The thief knew he is a thief. He likes to steal things. But you see he wasn't around the regular people. That's interesting isn't it? And why did he not hang around the regular people? Because the regular people either do not know who they are, at any given moment they could be anybody or someone else, and primary contradict by criticizing without examining their own lives and changing that which needs to be changed within.

At least those that are in power rather by force, coercion, or sheer cunning such as the self appointed illuminated elite at least they show you their true colors. They are showing you who they are. There is no faking. They say we are going to dominate society as long as you allow us to dominate, were going to suck the energy out of you, which is your money, your labor. You cannot get better than that, for a person to tell you who they are, to tell you what they are going to do, and to establish a tradition of doing this by publishing books, starting and ending wars and dictating how you live your life privately. What does humanity typically do or say? They say "That's not true, that person will change." Many have said that the supposed devil or the negative energy or the opposite polarity of you, you cannot change. It's destined to be who it is, so don't try. It's better that you get on being who you are, and get on doing what you need to do and let that energy continue to do what it needs to do. So the expectations that others have of you, the expectation to have this by a certain age, the expectations that you should be this, and that you are and you would be a failure if you don't have that. These are illnesses brought onto you that you have allowed and accepted by those who are ill themselves. So you are living out the fantasies or the horrors or joys that aren't even truly yours, because that's not what you would truly do if you had your own world to change any way you like.

Humanity at this point in reality is so ill that the earth herself has been overdosed with the blood of her inhabitants to the point that one who drinks too much alcohol is poisoned. Her poisoned state makes her weak, emotional, and deathly. Her born which are plants, trees, and such are in a weakened state and even in the best conditions are not producing the lifelong nutrients you would utilize normally to live a long and healthy life. As the energy of the earth is recognized and asserted as such through observation, your inner energy likewise is the same. If you are weak and polluting your temple with thoughts, actions, drinks, and smoke you are likely to be of the same.

The state of the body in conjunction with the spirit, soul, and the proper usage of mind, will you be able to achieve feats of the unbelievable. Strengthening your will by strengthening every faculty of yourself. Many want to talk about subjects out in other

41

galaxies, about beings that exist in other realms unheard of and it is fascinating, interesting, and intriguing to say the least. But what does that do for you? Nothing I presume, not a thing. It's a great story to hear things that other beings are doing in other universes or the other side of our galaxy or other dimensions. It's a great story, it's intriguing, it's interesting, and it's fascinating, it makes a good sci–fi story, it makes a good book, but it does absolutely nothing for you. What could that, hearing a story about the Pleiadians do for you? Nothing at all, and this is what these supposed illuminated ones laugh about. Because they feel humanity in general is like a spoiled, good for nothing, not naïve child. Because they can put out anything and it and the masses suck it up to be used psychologically as a form of escapism because their physical life seems inescapable.

You have your life to live, life is so precious it can be such a learning experience. You want to be Michael Jackson, but there is already a Michael Jackson. You want to be like these people who are themselves. Be you. We don't need any more Michael Jackson's. We don't need any more Muhammad Ali's. We have a Muhammad Ali's. We don't need any more Mansa Musa's. We have a Mansa Musa. But what about John Smith or Jane Doe or whatever your name may be? What about him, what about her? She needs to shine for better of humanity or worse of humanity. But at least she shines, that is the point. So wondering about these things does nothing.

Now would it be more fulfilling to reach this state or close to it on one's own? We are talking about the God state, the state of heavenly consciousness. Wouldn't it be great and absolutely fulfilling to reach that point on your own or at least get very close to it? And maybe someone would need to bring their hand down and pull you up. Everybody needs to be pulled up every once and a while and nothing is wrong with that. But for someone on level 1 to get handheld and personally assisted to level 100, that's a bit unreasonable. It would be more much more fulfilling and a wisdomatic learning experience to do so yourself. Then you could walk side by side with other divine beings instead of walking behind them permanently. And wanting someone to hold your hand, walk you where needed, and change your diaper while wiping you, no pun intended, you have literally forfeited your state as someone who will never be worthy of the way, worthy of praise, worthy of God saying we have another student who has overcome, now let's make him/her one of us. To be one of us, to be risen from the 33rd degree to 360th degree and beyond in whole-ness, in completeness.

Let's just say for arguments sake you want be part of the dark side, but the lessons move you more in line with the light. And you don't want to be part of the light; you want to be part of the dark. So you go that path, because it's quicker and it gets you to where you want to be. Like I said in previous lessons a woman would have sex with an animal, because it makes her an abomination. It makes her one that no man would choose to be with. Which absolutely degrades her and that's why they do that. Alester Crowley stated "Do what thou wilt shall be the whole of the law," not referencing sexuality entirely, impulses or physical actions, but more so the true you and what that true state wants to do, wants to accomplish.

During an outing with some the listeners during our meditation and walk through the forest preserve I showed them something in the sky that you wouldn't believe unless you seen it with your own eyes. Tomorrow I shall do the same with my thoughts which manifest in my actions and vibrate through my spirit. How will your spirit vibrate tomorrow? What if I said there is no tomorrow? There is only today. Life is only one long day. The lie was to get you to believe that each day symbolically is a separate and not directly linked to the next. That is why the youth today seem so insane in their actions and cannot fathom the consequences the next day because of such. If you literally live life like it's a long day instead of each day separate from the next you would be surprised what you could accomplish.

Exercise 5

The lessons for this week is to get into your car and as you are driving to the mall, a random store or where ever else picture a glowing flame in your hand. Picture it, as deeply red and as artistically as you can. It's a flame in your hand so visualize it getting brighter, stronger, and more powerful, let the fire in your hand burn from its brightness and strength. Imbrue it with the willed intention of getting you a good parking space. I want you to use this energy ball and practice getting parking spaces. The last component of it, as you visualize this flame in your hand, put your hand out and picture this energy just shooting out. Or you can just picture it floating from your hands going into the sky and kind of raining down on the parking lot. Don't be let down if it doesn't happen the first time. You will be surprised what happens. And then every time you go somewhere you get a desirable parking space, every single time. You will be surprised. Those who could see a lot further can see how this can be utilized for other things. No you cannot affect the direct will of a living soul in most circumstances just to answer that question for those who are students of the dark side. I know that's the first thing you want to do, is affect the will of others.

Lesson 6

Destroy Self,
Walk with thee Eternals

The letters in the alphabet are vibration signatures to a certain essence. The vibration is carried heavily with name that start with specific, which were common such as names that begin with O, X, or Z. Now many people of course in this time, typically name their children names from the biblical scriptures and things of this nature. Some of those names are powerful, magic notes, while others are not. And of course when you mix and match names, when you go esoterically into names and you have no research in doing so, the name itself could be a mixture of a goal and bad vibration. And so of course, some of you haved watched the movie 300 and it was supposedly the tale of the Spartans against the Kings of Kings, the God on Earth, from Persia, his name was Xerxes. When you go into certain periods of the time, certain letters are more prevalent in those times and it tells you what age and what they were vibrating to.

Who is your God or your governor? A magical note of destination of self is playing out in this reality. It destroys you from within. Some of the known notes are envy, jealousy, hatred, pity, anger, and so on and so forth. Each of the above has a frequency type which is of the ultra low type. Ultra low frequencies, when you feel hatred, when you feel anger, when you pity, show jealousy, or are envious. That's why people, who typically feel that way a lot of their life, typically suffer from an ailment. Also, you look at their skin, and even though they might be eating the right things, their skin still tells a tale. And that is because of these types of thoughts.

Now another devastating note that plays out for your ever immediate destination would be the non- supporting of the self-I. Self–I pertaining to all of self inwards and outwards, this would be called your goals, your aspirations. The one that observes this reality from the guarded seat on the outside the outside position viewing inward toward us, viewing inward toward those who are of the way.

THEE ETERNALS
1. Forever is the name, forever is the seat, forever without changes, without hatred, forever is the one,
2. The king of kings, the mystic of mystics, the master of masters,
3. The one who has taught me in all I know, and flows through me as I give this to you today,
4. The hierarchy of the one, from within you, from within the deepest of self, lies your seat upon a throne. Some of you have jesters and patrons of the courts,

46

5. While others sit alone, without any friends or family to talk to. Not even a jester, a fool to keep you company,

6. Seating alone looking into the abyss without a purpose or direction,

7. Without hearing and accepting the messenger,

8. In the shards of light that enter this world lays dimensions and realities un-told and unheard of. Realities where untold beings dwell but do not live as we do,

9. They're just some of the creations of the one not of the way,

10. The one who stepped off the path into the rough,

11. If you wonder he stepped to the left, left foot forward,

12. His creations vibrate in the realm of diabolical and disgust. He alone vibrates at an even number which is odd. In this world he allows seats to rotate but he will always control,

13. He is the adversary of the one,

14. He alone but with others of his kind weakened the one,

15. One of the last acts the one did,

16. The last act,

17. To vibrate thru all realities until the age of the one not of the path is over,

18. The one act which deserves a moment of silence....

19. ....

20. The last act in which all should bow their heads and be in observance,

21. Is life,

22. To allow all to live no matter how they vibrate, no matter for better or worse. To give reasoning for you to choose the right way in life,

23. The ability to live as I did and experience how it feels to be able to give life, to create life.

24. Meaning more plainly the act of bringing forth a child,

25. The pain to bring life,

26. It's the pain of the ultimate love,

27. The sacrifice I made for you,

-Divinely inspired from the teaching of the one, bestowed upon Priest T. A. Amen II on November 11th, 2012.

There was once a battle. And the battle was between the one and the adversary of the one. And in the battle, the one that was weakened had a last act but before that act at that time in this reality, life did not create as readily as we do today. The one literally harnessed the power of the internal universe within and expanded outright. And that's why the one's essence is literally everywhere. That is why you can see the Creator or the one in fish, insects, a tree, and obviously you can see the Creator in you and I. This was the last act, it was love. And of course the explosion of energy was painful to the one.

So spiritually, emotionally, physically and psychically is why woman go through so much pain to bring forth life. It is not a pain of disgust, it is not pain to purpose filled to put you on your knees, no, it is a pain of the ultimate love. The ultimate love that was developing within you. The ultimate love which was the gift. While even though the one is still around of course, but the one is in a guarded seat, in a different reality and projects thoughts to those in this reality that vibrate of a certain frequency. Now of course the being whose number is even, but seems odd, of course does not like this fact. Does not like that the one that he has defeated still is able to send messages through to this reality, some of those messages are absolutely divine, and some of these messages can make a common men king.

Exercise 6

And the lesson this week is no matter what, I want you to be yourself. Be yourself no matter what. Learn who you are. Learn the meanings of the lessons that you have been through in life. Learn what your path is and are you truly happy with it. Learn as you are the best that you are.

Now one who is full of folly would say I'm myself every day. Are you because if you have been watching TV since at least eight years, seven years old, and you're in your twenties now, more than likely you are not yourself. These are expert psychologists that work on those TV shows, those advertisements, to penetrate your mind.

Be who you are this week, find out who you are. Even if it stumps you, just sit there for hours and do it. I want you to be yourself no matter what. Some people change the way they are based on certain people in their environment to live up to, or to seem as if they are accustomed to whatever is going on. This is obviously a purposeful disillusion they are putting forth to appease whomever they feel deserves this betrayal to themselves.

Nothing is wrong for reaching high and wanting to be the best you that you can be, be do not betray you are truly because you only have to live with you in the end.

Lesson 7

The Nameless

The nameless... Are you ready to deal with reality? Are you ready to hear what you've been running away from? Are you ready to finally listen? What if what you hear, you will have to act in one way or another, because if you don't, if you don't act, the creator, the one, that governors this reality, the golden master's, the transcended ones, the ones guided by the masters and your fellow brothers and sisters down here in this world, they will all hold you personally responsible?

For listening, for hearing, for feeling the way of the one and purposely, with a certainty, turning your back on it. Some of you do not want to live in this world and going even deeper, many of you do not want to live in reality because of the diabolical nature of the current reality many of us create alternate realities to cope. Those who study psychology know what I am speaking of. But, they suffer from the same. One rather recent event would be California schools, which is in the united states allowing the children to chose which gender they are, which in turn they can go to the rest room of their choice based on their now, decided upon gender. So they are allowing children to govern children.

This is not a debate of gay vs. not, but rather a comment on what is reality and what is not. Do many of you believe children should, regardless of their born gender, decide what gender they really are? Do you believe that this is how reality should be? The demon, the Dracon, the opposing energy of reality, the trick is to give humanity such choices that anyone of sound mind would say are totally insane.

Regardless if you partake in those activities in private, at least those who take upon these activities in private would tell you that they would never do such things in public, why? Because they know that it's wrong, or goes against the workings of not just this reality, but goes against the nature of their makeup.

Some actions could be said as anti-humanity.

But the sad part is that humanity was once much wiser ages ago. Now humanity is so easily tricked. Humanity has lost its god head, or more best said its creator, its protector, its friend. And because humanity wanted to partake in the actions of the adversary, to take on the adversary as it's protector as it's friend, you get abortion clinics, children to change their sexual type, etc.

To treat people and to try to help people, within the insanity within this environment and to say they can or cannot be helped

51

based on the resources learned throughout your schooling, when you yourself are in the insanity regardless if you believe or not, is also insane.

The selfish yogi, he wants to leave this reality, he wants to be separate from you.

He left the cities where you dwell, where the vanity filled dwell, and escaped to solitude in the forest or jungles or the caves in mountains. He is there to reach the highest points in enlightenment to go to the other-verse, the anti-matter verse, or heaven. To de-materialize and become at worse one who has transcended, at best a golden master. Some of you seek this individual out, thinking, and hoping to be enlightened, but at best you have only disturbed the peace and internal growth of this yogi,

He is one of "The Nameless...."

There are those who are considered masters in every major and minor vortexed crystalined area in this world. There are also those who are governors who give these masters the divine guidance needed to keep these areas in a certain vibration state. For example, because you may live in New York, or California, or Chicago, or Atlanta it will not be destroyed. But if you were to leave these areas's it will fall out of balance, all because of you. The governors speak and in council get there guidance from the one who controls this cell. Based on alliances and allegiances to the past one who controlled this cell some speak to you in dreams, some guide you through life.

Some keep you nameless amongst the named.

Keeping you on a ever path of growth and development so that you may grow to the next level within this cell or move on to the other-world, the anti-matter world, or the higher heavens to dwell there. So in has without learning your lessons, your lessons that will prepare you for the next world, the higher heavens, or to be born again in higher positions of influence spiritually, you act in hast.

Every not patient to follow the way....

The way the one has set forth for your life, for you to learn and journey forward. Even the universe was created by an act, a quite dramatic one at that. The yogi, the selfish yogi in the mountain lies to you. He lies to you because of his own self preservation motives. Please hear me, not all, but some. He tells you to be, don't ruffle feathers, be at peace, and be ever forgiving, which are all true statements, but the yogi is hoping you will not do one great thing; this thing would be an act. Do I mean an act of violence? An act could be as easy as a non-act, in the non-act there is action, an example would be you work for a company and you find that this company is doing negative things around the world, against the helpless people of the world, that you do not agree with. You are in a descent position at work where if you just stopped it would be turmoil.

So you just stop,

You do nothing,

You dwell in nothingness within the confined space of the chaos that consumes that companies actions worldwide. Now think about if 10 employees did this, what about 40, what about 100?

What if all of you did this?

So in non-action there is more power than actually action. Some of you were in the military and since the machines don't drive themselves, at least not yet, what if you did nothing, what if everyone did nothing?

Guess what? Then nothing would happen.

There would be an external state of nothingness.

One that reflects that ever-inner-nothing-filled-state-within.

This state is what angers the one who controls this world the most. He, in reference to the energy there of, is in a ever state of chaotic-propulsion, ever chaotically moving forward in chaos to create order out of the chaos. Once the plan has been completed, the plan to control this sphere, this world, this cell, because in controlling this cell, you control the atum.

This cells, cells, meaning you and I once created beings on this cell with great wisdom and strength.. Since they were ever guided by the stars which are guided by the one, but now the cells are born weak, they are born by parents who have yet to gain any wisdom or understanding. Some cells are destroyed before even getting a chance to try to strengthen this cell.

What do i mean by this statement? It means abortions.

Even many cells within this cell… within the body of the one have even stopped duplicating themselves, even stopped the whole physical purpose, which is to continue on, to strengthen or weaken the one. But that choice has yet to even occur, why? Because of homosexuality.

There is a deeper understanding and reasoning to all that happens around you all that takes place within your visual sphere. Do not take anything or everything as lightly. The reason many of you tend to not be able to keep secrets and be ever willing to speak your thoughts and emotions, is not because they trained you to do so via some type of enslavement, mind control, No, they are not that exact, that powerful atleast not yet, it's in fact because of the inner communication between cells, you long for telling all that you know, which in turn the next cell will do the same until all are in unison.

Until all are one, which is the natural state.

Those of you who are ever vigilant in your studying of the lessons, who are ever vigilant in your tea's and meditation, ever vigilant in your forgiveness of self, and your powering up of your will, ever forgiving in your forgiveness of others, ever supporting of the self-I. You should be wary of speaking your thoughts out loud; the ether picks them up and they propagate around the ionosphere. An example is how you may think of an idea so unique, so refined, defined and perfected and then at the same time and you speak it out in excitement. Then mysteriously someone on the other side of the world comes up with the exact same thought, and then it becomes who will be the first to bring it forth.

In the past this was a future event, in the present we are, I am ever present, in the future…. who are listening now, listen to the ones direction from the past.

Exercise 7

Exercise this week is three parts, listen closely

First… on Tuesday, starting this upcoming Tuesday at 10pm c.s.t. which is 9pm pst or 11pm est we will do a worldwide group meditation. At the same time across the globe.

Please seat in silence if your able….for at least just 5minutes sending love to the one, sending love to the world, sending love through this universe.

In doing so the earth will brighten and she shall be seen from eons away. Those who see this brightness will come and visit. Many of you who want to see… want to see something in the physical that you have yet to see? Well, this will start the process of processes. Be ever ready.

The 2nd part is a meditation on Thursday @ 10pm c.s.t. you will just meditate in silence for at least 11 minutes. Just 11 minutes you will meditate preferably with a cleared mind.

In this myself and some of the masters of this world will be increasing your inner psycho, increasing the connection between this verse and the next, increasing the vibration state of all of you who are listening and who will partake in this exercise.

This will be a one-time event on Thursday December 20th 2012 @ 10pm.

@ 11pm on December 20th 2012, we will all meditate on the healing of the great mother, the one who sustains us all. The one who protects us with her shield, the one who feeds us with her flesh, the earth! It shall be an earth healing meditation for at least 7minutes starting at 11pm c.s.t. on dec 20th 2012

Those in the past who are listening, I look forward to your participation, those in the present bear witness to the self-I, and those in the future, these are the events that have transpired before your time that have allowed those things we know to be.